Kid from Kauai

First Printing, April 2002
1 2 3 4 5 6 7 8 9

Design: Carol Colbath

ISBN 1-56647-536-8

Mutual Publishing
1215 Center Street, Suite 210
Honolulu, Hawai'i 96816
Ph: (808) 732-1709
Fax: (808) 734-4094
e-mail: mutual@lava.net
www.mutualpublishing.com

Printed in Korea

Kid from Kauai

A Memoir

By Robert Okazaki
and Dorothy Hazzard

Martha Hazzard Press

HONOLULU HAWAII
2001

Foreword

This memoir is dedicated to the three most important women in Bob's life: his mother, Yoshi; his wife, Shizuko; and his daughter, Martha-Ann.

THE HAWAIIAN ISLANDS

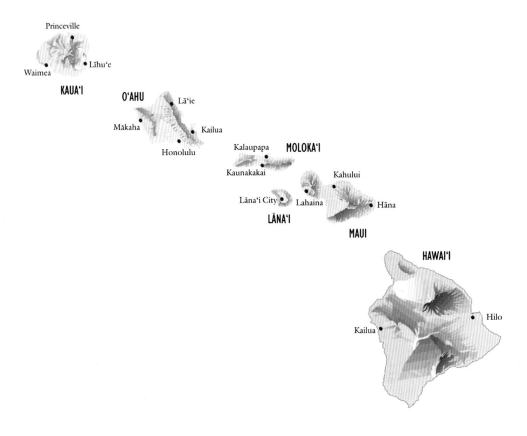

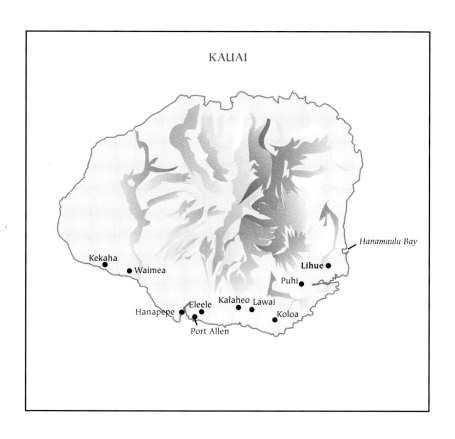

KAUAI

Kekaha

Waimea

Hanamaulu Bay

Lihue

Puhi

Kalaheo Lawai

Eleele

Hanapepe

Koloa

Port Allen

Contents

CHAPTER 1

HAWAIIAN HUCKLEBERRY FINN

There are few among us who have survived moray eel bites, ghosts, four major wars, a depression, breadlines, dangerous jobs, broken bones, drunken sprees, jail, rednecks, ship collisions, earthquakes, tidal waves, two wives, countless girlfriends, success and failure, plus life's extreme highs and lows. Bob Okazaki experienced them all, and lived to tell of it.

If you could bottle and sell his stamina, you'd be a billionaire.

It all began in the late 1800's when a courageous young married couple emigrated from Japan to Hawaii, to work on a sugar plantation near Lihue, Kauai. They came from the Yamaguchi-Ken prefecture. Their names were Naokichi and Yoshi Okazaki. They lived in the plantation camp at Hanamaulu, along with the other contract laborers. Both husband and wife worked in the cane fields, as was the custom then. Neither ever learned to speak English.

Their home was a rustic cottage. Robert Tomoichi Okazaki was born there on October 20, 1910, second from the youngest of ten children. (Among them was a set of triplets.) Life was very different from today, and these are some of his memories.

Part of the house had a board floor. But the kitchen's floor was hard-packed dirt. The family ate there on a crudely built table. There was a sort of fireplace for a stove, with two holes in which to place cooking pots. No oven, no bread or cookies. Little meat or fish. Plenty of vegetables and rice. Indeed, there were acres of rice paddies in the valley, and water buffaloes still in use at the time.

Bob loved to go to his "Portagee" friends' homes because of their delicious bread. The Portuguese were "lunas," supervisors on the sugar plantations. Their status was higher. So each family was given a better house, an outdoor oven, and an acre of land. They were generous to the small hungry boy, knowing he considered bread a luxury.

There was no refrigeration in the plantation camp kitchens; the ice box came later. A screened cupboard held supplies and leftovers. There was no electricity at first; only kerosene lamps. They did have running water, such as it was. When tiny fish and frogs came tumbling out, they used Bull Durham tobacco bags for faucet filters.

The sleeping area was on a different level, with tatami mats spread on the wooden floor. Everyone slept there, on top of "futons" (thin, quiltlike Japanese mattresses), covered by more futons.

The cottage was of single wall construction, with open cracks between slats. Bob often helped with major

Bob's parents were married in Japan before emigrating to Hawaii in the late 1800s. Japanese wedding attire of the era.

The Okazaki family around 1917. Left to right: Ume, one of two surviving triplets; mother Yoshi; Seichi, who was sent to Japan to be raised by his grandparents; Omitsu; father Naokichi; Bob; and Omatsu, the other triplet. Four more older children were probably away working. Father and sons wore Western style clothing for this formal photo session.

home improvement projects. They papered the walls and ceilings with newspapers, pasted on with a mixture of flour, water and chili pepper to discourage bugs. New layers were added over the years. They didn't call it recycling then, more like redecorating. Practical, too; it made the house tighter, kept out mosquitoes, and looked better than bare boards. In the night, as the layers of newspaper aged and loosened, Bob could hear geckoes running around inside.

It was a time when they still had outhouses, crude sheds some distance from the cottages. Inside was a plank bench with a hole cut into it for a toilet. A hole big enough to sit on but not large enough to fall through. Toilet paper? No such thing. Newspaper had to do.

A six-foot-deep pit beneath the outhouse received the excrement which was sprinkled with lime occasionally as a sanitary measure. After a while, the pit became pretty ripe. When it got too full, they simply moved the outhouse to a different spot and covered the pit with fresh dirt. These privies existed everywhere in the world, not just in Hawaii, in one form or another, well into the twentieth century.

Some of the camps had communal, unisex outhouses with as many as six holes. Boys, girls, men and women used them together as needed. They sometimes chatted pleasantly as they sat there, doing their business; it all seemed perfectly natural. The Japanese were totally unselfconscious about bodily functions, and remained so when they emigrated to Hawaii.

The Okazaki family shared a two-holer with a neighbor. Bob was terrified if he had to go in the night. He woke up his mother and begged her to accompany him. It was because of the "obake," ghosts featured in Japanese stories and movies. Parents, including Yoshi, routinely threatened their children with the dread obake to make them behave. Mysterious accidents, illnesses, bad luck, curses, losses—all were blamed on the obake.

What did these ghosts look like, assuming you could see them? Sort of like Western ghosts except that they couldn't walk or run because they had no legs. They wore spooky greyish, whitish garments like long dresses and glided along. Animals could see the obake, even if humans could not. Dogs were especially sensitive.

A man from Japanese stores outside the camps came by on horseback in the evenings to take orders for next day deliveries. One time he assured Bob and the other impressionable kids that his horse had seen an obake, and reared up in fright, nearly bucking him off. He made it a breathtaking tale. Given his vivid imagination, poor Bob got the willies. He knew ghosts were lurking everywhere. Definitely in graveyards. No amount of money could have induced him to enter, or even pass by, a graveyard at night.

The man enjoyed scaring the kids so much he held them spellbound with another story. To appreciate this one, you have to realize that, back then, children and adults in the plantation camps still wore Japanese clothing.

Three men were drinking and bragging about how fearless they were. A wager developed. They dared each other to go into the graveyard at night, one at a time. To prove he had really done it, each man would take a

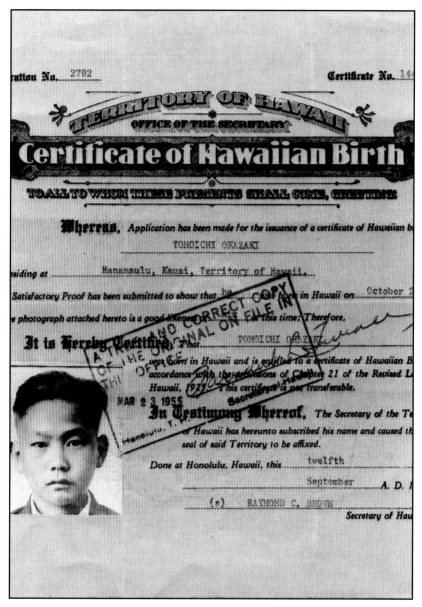

Bob's birth certificate was issued nearly 15 years after he was born, by the Territory of Hawaii. He was second from the youngest of 10 children.

marked stake to drive into the ground at a certain grave located well inside the cemetery. The others would check the next day to see if the stake were there. Money was pooled. Whoever bravely overcame his fear of ghosts, and proved it, could share the kitty. Each secretly expected to win it all.

The first man summoned up his nerve, took his stake, went into the graveyard that night and eventually came back out, shaken but still alive. Next day they found he had indeed planted his stake in the right place. Same thing with the second man the second night.

The third man went in the third night, but never returned. The others waited all night, getting more apprehensive by the minute. By dawn's early light, they rushed in and found him dead on the correct grave.

"The obake got him!"

"It could have been us!"

"What have we done?"

"We were fools to challenge the ghosts!"

When the two men finally stopped berating themselves, they took a closer look. Their friend had reached the right grave, all right, and had driven in his stake. But he had accidentally driven it through a corner of his kimono, pinning himself to the grave. Thinking he was in the clutches of an obake, the superstitious fellow had died of fright.

Now Bob had a serious case of the heebie-jeebies, on top of the willies!

He went to English school as soon as he was old enough, and then to Japanese school afterwards every day. One of the classes at the English school was gardening for an hour a day. Each pupil was given a four-by-ten-foot bed of soil to plant with vegetables. They took part in islandwide competitions for the best school gardens. Teachers also inspected home gardens to see how well the students were applying what they had been taught.

The school held an essay contest every week. Winners got much coveted stars on the blackboard. Though Bob didn't actually win a contest, his best subject was geography. A difficulty was that his parents spoke no English, and couldn't relate very well to his school work. An advantage was that he grew up bilingual.

The teachers had ingenious ways to stimulate learning. On a phonograph, they played opening measures of operatic tunes, and held "Guess That Song" contests. There were also regular singing lessons.

Sports included barefoot football, played in school leagues. Bob finally grew to 125 lbs. and was eligible for the minimum weight category.

Practically every day, Bob and the other boys would head for the beach after school. They put together their own slings and goggles, and persuaded a blacksmith to make them spears. Then they dove, holding their breath for as long as a whole minute, spearing fish which they later "threw on the fire" on the beach, and ate.

Meanwhile, back at home, the family raised chickens which ran free, and pigs in a pen out back, near a ditch full of running water. Eventually, they built chicken and rabbit coops. Thus they added meat to the head

Everyone feared the "obake," ghosts in the cemetery, who caused mysterious accidents, illnesses, bad luck, curses, losses—and worse.

The boys swam in the river, pulling themselves along in tunnels in the thick buffalo grass which grew beside the banks.

cabbages, tomatoes, yams, eggplants, green beans and other vegetables from the home garden.

By age 12, during school vacations, Bob and his pals worked in the cane fields for 25 cents a day. They hoed weeds along the troughs of "pula-pula," newly planted (by hand) sugar cane cuttings. Sure enough, they were terrorized by legendary fierce lunas equipped with whips and sticks.

Bob and his friends always brought their lunch to work. His consisted of rice, rice and more rice, with fried eggplant or burdock. Somehow the boys found time to swim in the river, pulling themselves along in tunnels in the thick buffalo grass which grew beside the banks.

What happened to Bob's formal education? In grape season, he and some other boys got jobs trampling ripe grapes in big tubs, with their bare feet. The grapes were grown on arbors by the Portuguese who were preparing to make wine which they always had available in barrels. Unfortunately, when no one was looking, Bob and a couple of other boys sampled the wine from an unguarded barrel and got very, very drunk. Not only did they lose their jobs with the grapes, but they got kicked out of school.

So it was back to the beach with the merry outcasts for hours of spear fishing, crabbing and lobstering. He remembers diving into underwater caves and pulling "tabi" (slipper) lobsters off the underside of the cave ceiling, two and three at a time. The boys gave away part of their catches, brought some home, and sold the rest.

Where sand crabs had dug holes in the beach, and

Where sand crabs had dug holes in the beach, and were hiding too deeply for the boys to dig out, they tricked the creatures instead.

were hiding too deeply for the boys to dig out, they put gravity to work, tricking the creatures instead. They planted open pails in the beach, keeping the tops flush with the sand itself, and left them overnight. After dark, the crabs became active, crept out of hiding, and fell into the pails. The sides were too vertical and slippery for them to crawl out. All the boys had to do was go back at dawn, gather up crabs by the pailful, and make a fire on the beach to enjoy a boiled crab breakfast.

As for school, once he tasted the carefree life for a boy on Kauai in those days, Bob never went back.

CHAPTER 2

ENDLESS SUMMER

In his early teens, Bob got another job in the cane fields, a much better job paying 75 cents a day instead of 25. This was for an experimental agricultural station on Kauai. Bob was part of a team of three boys and a foreman. They measured the cane, "knuckle to knuckle," for rate of growth. Red ribbons and small knicks marked where they had left off. The foreman compared previous marks, wrote down the results and reported to the station's lab.

His father had died when Bob was only 10, leaving Yoshi to raise all those children herself. Bob didn't hesitate to turn over his pay to his busy mother. She in return gave him an allowance of 25 cents a week. Bob said you could do a lot with 25 cents in those days.

It didn't cost anything to play with marbles. Coconuts, bananas, papayas, mangoes, guava and mountain apples were free for the plucking. Bob earned free tickets to the weekly Japanese shows by passing out advertising flyers. He remembered the colorful banners and exciting Japanese drumming. Most impressive was a performer who put on one-man shows, bewitching the audience with his range of different voices. Popular silent pictures, costing only a few pennies for admission, were shown outdoors at first, later in a real theater with benches.

Bob recalled roaming the forest with his chums. They knocked down wild wasps' nests, often getting stung in the process, turning up next day with swollen faces and eyes. What in the world were they after? Larvae, fat, squirming white critters an inch long. Others were ready to hatch, complete with tiny wings and legs. These delicacies, something like shrimp, were cooked in the woods over a small fire and eaten with shoyu and sugar. Not with the fingers, either, but with civilized chopsticks.

While the plantation gave widowed Yoshi free use of the house, and she worked for a pittance in the cane fields, she knew she had to earn extra income. She worked as a midwife for the camp. She sometimes cooked for more prosperous households. She enlisted the children's help with another project, making tofu in five gallon cans and selling it around the neighborhood. Bob did his share of cranking the primitive equipment used in preparing the soy bean curd.

At first, the contract laborers had expected to return to Japan, but few ever did. In fact, Yoshi took Bob's younger brother to Japan and left him with her parents to raise, a custom with the Japanese in Hawaii at the time. He didn't speak a word of English when she brought him back 12 years later. One by one, his sisters moved to Honolulu, working as maids, lessening the economic pressure on their mother.

Mother Yoshi, widowed when Bob was 10, kept house, raised the children, worked in the cane fields, acted as midwife, made and sold tofu, and sometimes cooked for more prosperous households.

A rare treat was when Yoshi took Bob to Oahu, traveling steerage class on a small interisland steamer. They enjoyed a month's vacation visiting friends and relatives. Honolulu seemed like New York City, London and Paris combined to the impressionable kid from Kauai. Waikiki was as enticing then as now, perhaps more so. Bob was impressed when shown stately homes and gardens by family friends who worked as yard men for the upper crust "haoles" (Caucasians or white persons).

There was an extended period when Bob didn't work, his mother supported him, and he went to the beach every day. He drank a lot, fished a lot, and went through a kind of identity crisis.

The girls he had always taken for granted, bathing naked with them in Japanese style "furos" (deep communal bathtubs), began to look extremely interesting. And they were not bashful. There were plenty of adolescent boy-girl shenanigans in the cane fields to distract him.

The furos were large wooden tubs with metal bottoms, raised to make room for a fire beneath. The Japanese liked their water hot, hotter, hottest! Your feet were kept from burning by a wooden grill on top of the metal floor.

Bob's fishing got more sophisticated. He and his friends would circle around Hanamaulu Bay in a rowboat full of gill nets. One boy, the "kilo" (close observer), would climb the surrounding cliffs, looking down into the water, spotting schools of akule with their red backs and mullet which jumped and splashed. You couldn't see them so well down at sea level.

The instant the boys in the boat got his signal, they circled the fish with the gill nets, and dove down to tie the ends securely. Then they would spank the water violently with a big lauhala stump, scaring the fish into the nets where they became entangled. The nets were pulled up, fish and all. Sometimes Bob had to dive again to free the nets caught on coral. Then he had to evade sharks who were attracted by the commotion.

An alternate way of fishing was to hold a "hukilau" (seine fishing event). Villagers gathered on the beach and helped Bob and the others pull up a big netful of akule and bring it ashore. Everyone pitched in and freed the fish from the net, tossing them into a heap on the sand. The boss then divided the catch, awarding tasty, big-eyed fish to this person and that, ending up with half a dozen to a family.

At dusk, Bob and the boys would lay nets they had made themselves out of soft cord to catch lobsters. Lead weights kept the bottoms down and floaters kept the tops up, so the nets were held upright in the water, parallel to each other, around 20 feet apart. In the night, the lobsters became entangled in the nets and the boys plucked them off in the morning.

They speared squid at a rocky beach with shallow water. Bob's hand got badly bitten by a vicious moray eel when he reached into a hole where he thought a squid was hiding. He bore the scars for the rest of his life.

Early on, he learned how to pick "opihi," the small, oval-shaped limpets prized by native Hawaiians. If he so much as touched their shells, they gripped the rocks and were impossible to pry loose. Instead, he slipped his knife beneath them quickly, before they knew what was happening, and off they came.

For a couple of years, Bob worked as a blacksmith's helper on Kauai, in a busy shop with five forges, and several skilled men from whom he learned to handle red hot steel. They fabricated metal objects, shod horses, and even welded large pieces of equipment like railroad axles.

He didn't know it then, but it was an education in the properties of metal that would prove valuable to him later.

CHAPTER 3

SHIPPING OUT

Against his mother's wishes, when he was 19, Bob impetuously joined the Merchant Marine. His main objective was to visit the fleshpots of San Francisco, which a friend had been describing to him in living color.

He signed onboard a ship carrying sugar from Kauai to the Mainland and bringing back lumber to Hawaii. The ship needed six able-bodied seamen (ABs) for the trip to comply with a union contract, so they grabbed him to fill out the roster. It was a stretch, because he knew virtually nothing about the job.

All his life, Bob plunged in and learned by doing, surviving as best he could. He was a quick study. This way he gained a remarkable assortment of skills and experience. He liked living on the edge, and couldn't resist dangerous challenges, from Alaska to Panama and South America; through the Panama Canal to New York City.

But he became so seasick on his first voyage, before he even left Hawaiian waters, he wanted to die. He almost jumped ship. The seasoned seamen encouraged him to stick it out and he surprised himself by living. Away they sailed to the West Coast, a 14-day trip. After a couple of days he was never seasick again.

In those days, cattle boats delivered the creatures to the different islands. Where there were no docks, they anchored offshore and the ranchers drove the bewildered cattle into the water, forcing them to swim to the ship. Then they were winched onboard through the air in slings, one by one, an unpleasantly thrilling experience for a cow.

Our hero worked watches (shifts) with a partner. His quartermaster duties meant working a watch in the wheelhouse, steering the ship for hours on end, focusing on the compass intently, while the partner stayed outside on the bridge, acting as lookout.

As they neared land, Bob steered under the watchful eye of the captain who would call out commands:

"Port rudder!"

"Starboard rudder!"

"Straight ahead!"

"Ease it up!"

"Steady it up!"

Deckhand jobs were endless for an AB, and he learned them all. Maintenance work included splicing rope, scraping, painting—odds and ends everywhere to keep the vessel shipshape.

He got to know the difference between a river pilot and a harbor pilot. And learned that a Jacob's ladder had nothing to do with heaven; the pilots used it to climb up and down the ship's side.

When he was 19, Bob impetuously joined the Merchant Marine.
He signed onboard a ship carrying sugar from Kauai to the Mainland.

San Francisco met and even exceeded his expectations. The ship then sailed to the Columbia River, the boundary between Washington and Oregon. A river pilot met them at the Astoria Bar, a famous sand bar at the river's mouth. It could be foggy and stormy there, with treacherous currents.

They sailed up the river, unloaded sugar at St. Helen's, and loaded lumber. Bob loved the action, and voyaged many times in his life with the Merchant Marine whenever he felt the call of the sea.

Now Yoshi, his mother, was determined that he should settle down and become a solid citizen. When he returned from his first voyage, she persuaded him to to stay ashore and get a job, which he did, as a quarry laborer in Honolulu, where the University of Hawaii's stadium was built later. The heavy equipment included a big drill and a derrick with a 20-foot tower. He did site preparation on the cliffs for the machines. Rock was dynamited, broken into big chunks, or crushed. It was hot, dusty, dangerous work, but it was a regular job.

That was all Yoshi needed to get busy and arrange a marriage for her darling son, to a nice local girl. Sort of an old-fashioned "picture bride" affair. In the Japanese tradition, his new wife insisted that he learn a trade, so he went to welding school for a few months. It turned out to be a brief marriage, as the two barely knew each other, and Bob wasn't ready for matrimony. He had too many adventures ahead of him, and soon went back to sea, abandoning his bride, probably to her relief.

When his ship entered foggy Puget Sound, on its way to Seattle, Bob was lookout on the bow. He manned a bell, signaling the helmsman, ringing once to bear port, twice to bear starboard, three times for straight ahead. When the crew went ashore in Seattle, it was wine, women and song night and day.

The north Pacific was known for its heavy seas. The worst waves he encountered were from 20 to 30 feet high. Once, his ship lost its forward mast and was lucky to limp back to Honolulu. Shipboard work continued, though, rain or shine. In addition to scouring and painting all surfaces, Bob had to climb a smokestack to shine the ship's whistle, dangling in a bosun's chair. Below deck, he had to coil the huge anchor chain, one of the most hazardous jobs on the ship. You could lose a leg if it got caught in the chain when it was being winched in as they were retrieving the anchor.

One foggy night, Bob was lookout on a ship leaving the Columbia River. It was headed out with a load of lumber and the river pilot was already on board. Suddenly, off the port bow, a big shape loomed up! He realized instantly it was on a collision course with his ship, and frantically rang the warning bell. He stayed in position, risking being crushed. In seconds, his ship swung about to avoid the other, but there was a tremendous crash as the bow smashed into the side of Bob's ship. Both vessels were badly damaged.

It could have been worse. If the *Rialto*, from Italy, had struck the engine room, instead of the aft midship section, chances are Bob's ship would have sunk. They had lifeboats at the ready. Instead, the load of lumber absorbed much of the impact, and helped keep the ship afloat, though it was perilously low in the water.

Bob at 19, ready to go ashore and visit the fleshpots of San Francisco.

They made it to a shipyard upriver and went into dry dock. Who should they find in the neighboring dry dock? The *Rialto*! The Italian sailors proved friendly. They introduced Bob and his shipmates to cognac. While waiting for the repairs, they partied together. Maybe a little too much. It wasn't the first time the captain had to bail his men out of jail.

During another voyage, Bob was "on the wheel," steering the ship as it entered Hanamaulu Harbor on Kauai where he had fished and swum for years. They were picking up a load of sugar at Ahukini Landing.

The captain was an arrogant German who, in a fit of overconfidence, had not requested a harbor pilot. He thought he could do it himself. Consequently, he kept shouting out commands Bob knew were wrong. But under no circumstances could he disobey the captain. Talk about being between a rock and a hard place! He braced himself for the worst.

First, they went too far in, to where it was getting shallow, and nearly ran aground. Second, they turned too widely, and nearly smashed into the pier. Third, they stopped just in time, backed up, and then went full speed ahead, almost crashing into the breakwater. Finally, they managed to dock safely, barely averting three serious accidents.

Back on Kauai, between voyages, Bob got another risky job, building water tunnels through the mountains for the plantations. Surveyors and engineers directed the project. Bob helped excavate the dirt, lay railway tracks as they went deeper, and load the dirt in carts which rolled it away. They shored up the soft places on the walls and ceilings with timber, but there were still cave-ins and several accidental deaths.

Deep inside the tunnels, the surveyors used candle-light shadows to determine direction, a primitive but effective method.

A foreman's house near the job site provided room and board for Bob and a group of friendly Filipinos who caught frogs for "pupus" (snacks) at night. They also sneaked up on large sleeping doves in mango trees and shot them for dinner. They shared their potent home made brew called "swipe" with Bob, playing the ukulele and singing the night away.

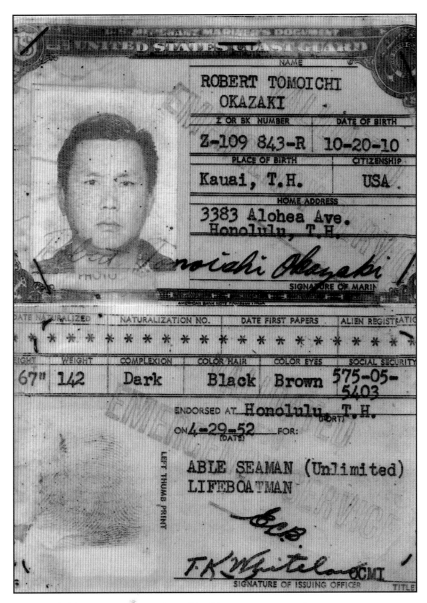

His AB (Able Seaman) card enabled him to sign on for many voyages with the Merchant Marine.

Leaving the Columbia River in a thick fog, Bob's ship collided with the *Rialto*, from Italy. Neither ship sank, but both were badly damaged.

CHAPTER 4

THE GREAT DEPRESSION

The stock market crash of 1929 found Bob stranded in Seattle—"on the beach," as they called it in the Merchant Marine. Thousands of people were out of work, many on the verge of starvation. They had to scramble to stay alive. Desperate times called for desperate measures.

Bob resorted to standing in bread lines for food, along with hundreds of others. It was humiliating, but everyone was in the same boat.

Luckily for him, he ran into some Hawaiians. They were veteran Alaskan fishermen who lived in Seattle during the off-season for salmon, which was winter in the "Lower 48." They took in their Hawaiian "brah" (brother) and let him sleep on the floor of their housekeeping room in Chinatown. He knew he was in good hands when he saw four or five huge bags of rice in their quarters.

He had no money and wracked his brain for a way to repay their generosity. He and a friend went to the fish market every day and picked up discarded salmon heads. He knew they still had good meat on the "cheeks."

Back at the room, they boiled the heads with salt, made flour "poi," (a paste usually made from Hawaiian taro corms), and shared this makeshift diet with their Hawaiian benefactors. Contributing like this helped relieve his acute sense of obligation, not to mention his hunger.

"The worst times make the best friends," said Bob.

Next, glad to get any job, he became a migrant worker. He was recruited to pick hops in Moxee City, near Yakima, by Filipinos who drove him across the state in the dark of night. The vines grew on wires stretched between 10-foot posts. Using both hands at once, they picked only the small white flowers, which were then dried in a kiln. This work paid two cents a pound. Bob almost got fired; for the first two days he picked leaves and stems by mistake, along with the flowers, trying to build up the poundage.

The workers slept in a barn's hayloft, with smelly cattle below. It was Bob's first experience with such a structure; until then, he had never really seen a barn. They ate in Filipino kitchens, which served lots of rice and pumpkin every day, with tiny bits of pork and vegetables. A gourmet cuisine after the Seattle breadlines.

At night, Bob joined the men who drove out into the countryside to hunt jack rabbits in the sagebrush. The rabbits froze when caught in the car headlights. Bang! They were shot. Bob never forgot how they jumped 10 feet in the air in a death throe spasm when they were killed. The men skinned and cleaned the animals, roast-

In the Great Depression, Bob became a migrant worker picking apples in Wenatchee, Washington, where two famous pilots landed, completing the first nonstop flight from Asia to the U.S. Mainland.

ed them in a kiln, and feasted on the welcome change of diet.

As different crops ripened, the migrant workers moved on to help with the harvest. After the hops, it was apples in Wenatchee. He earned four cents a box and, hungry for work, picked the most from the first day. He quickly learned to use both hands at once, carefully leaving the stem on the apples. Otherwise, the fruit might rot. There were several varieties; Delicious and Winesap stuck in his memory. They called the riper apples "colored," and they picked only the right colors.

The atmosphere was threatening for migrant workers up and down the West Coast. The local rednecks hated them for taking what they considered their jobs. There had been assaults, murders and incidents of arson in California. At night, armed guards patrolled the barracks where the workers slept, protection provided by the orchard owners.

In 1931, a historic event took place in Wenatchee when famous pilots Pangborn and Herndon landed at the local airport, completing the very first nonstop flight from Asia to the U.S. Mainland. Bob was thrilled to be there. The airport was named after Pangborn later on.

These jobs paid so little, Bob had no money for transportation back to Seattle when they ended. He then became a hobo, joining a roving brotherhood since celebrated in story and song. While waiting for a train, the men buried themselves in lumber yard sawdust, up to their necks, to keep warm. When they heard the train coming, they popped out, raced to the tracks, careful to avoid the railroad "bulls" (security men), caught the train, and hid in refrigerator car vents all the way back to Seattle.

Bob eked out a living during the Depression years by taking any jobs he could get in Washington and Hawaii. These included working for his meals in a Japanese restaurant, and as a jackhammer operator on the breakwater at Port Allen, Kauai.

As an AB, or able-bodied seaman, he made a 45-day "Pineapple Run" on the S. S. *Makawao,* a Matson cargo ship which came into Port Allen. At times, he sailed on other ships under the Golden Gate Bridge to San Francisco, Alameda, and the Crockett sugar refinery in the Bay area. It was wine, women and song all over again when they went ashore.

The country perked up after Franklin Roosevelt was elected president in 1932. He swung into action to fight the Depression with progressive programs under the New Deal. One of his innovations was the Civilian Conservation Corps, or CCC, which put young men to work in useful projects around the country.

Bob applied for a job in Kokee, Kauai, at a CCC camp near Waimea Canyon. He expected to be clearing trails and planting trees, but the CCC made him one of three camp cooks feeding a hundred people a day.

He took this challenge in his stride and studied a cookbook on large-scale meals. Sometimes he cooked Japanese food for the men who came from all different parts of the country and had never tasted it. He found they loved it. He was glad to turn over most of his pay to his mother.

News was ominous in the late 1930s, and people felt

Bob, left, with CCC buddies.

CCC camp at Kokee, Kauai, where Bob became one of three camp
cooks. The Civilian Conservation Corps put young men to work in
useful projects around the country.

war was coming. Bob joined the Army National Guard, dying to see some action as a machine gunner. He was stationed at Schofield Barracks in Central Oahu. Captain Duval, his old boss from the CCC, was brought in to train the first draftees. The captain said "No way!" to Bob's goal of machine gunning, and insisted he was too good a cook. At least Bob had the satisfaction of teaching the other military cooks to prepare rice properly. The pots were so large, they had been leaving it raw in the middle.

Bob was honorably discharged in November, 1941, because he had a dependent mother. He immediately got a job as a welder with the Pacific Naval Air Base, contractors for a dredging project at—of all the fateful places and times!—*Pearl Harbor.*

CHAPTER 5

PEARL HARBOR

A launch picked up Bob and a dozen other workers and took them out to the dredge near Pearl Harbor's mouth. It was a big modified barge which held heavy specialized equipment designed to suck the mud out of shallow places in the harbor and deposit it as landfill on Ewa plain. The channels had to be kept open so the ships wouldn't run aground.

There was a submarine net across the harbor's entrance that supposedly made it impregnable. Mighty battleships were lined up in an impressive row farther inside the harbor, across from the naval shipyard, one of the biggest and busiest in the country.

Early on Sunday morning, December 7, 1941, Bob went to work as usual, weekend or no weekend. He had just stepped off the launch and was storing his lunch inside when he heard planes zooming in from the Waianae Mountains on West Oahu. Lots of planes, flying low, too low, really. In the noise and confusion, Bob didn't realize they were under Japanese attack until bullets rained down as the planes began strafing just past the dredge. Then he spotted the rising sun insignias and knew they were Zeroes. They were heading for the battleships around the bend from where he was standing. Everyone was in shock, it happened so fast.

The men on the dredge weren't armed and didn't know what to do. They could hear the fearful explosions as torpedoes struck the battleships. They could see thick smoke rising, and planes wheeling around, strafing the shipyard, then flying away.

Bob saw what were later known as "kamikazes." These were attacks by an elite corps of young, idealistic Japanese pilots trained for suicidal missions against American battleships. At Pearl Harbor, he watched some planes dive straight into ship smokestacks and explode. The uproar and destruction were frightful.

The kamikazes had written poignant farewells to their loved ones before setting off on their missions, fully aware they faced certain death, which they considered honorable. They were similar to the gladiators in ancient Rome who said, "We who are about to die salute thee."

They eventually sank hundreds of U.S. ships, mostly around Midway and Okinawa. It was nearly impossible to put up a defense against such fanaticism.

During the Pearl Harbor attack, the Americans finally manned their antiaircraft guns and fought back. One damaged Japanese plane plunged headfirst into the mud near Bob's dredge. They could see two pilots' heads sticking up out of the water. A couple of his fellow workers grabbed crowbars, and rushed over in a rowboat to kill the enemy. When they got there, they found only bloody water in the wreckage. They assumed the pilots had dove down and committed "hari-kari" (Japanese suicide). The bodies were never found.

A destroyer managed to get underway and spied a tiny, two-man Japanese submarine entering the harbor, near Bob's dredge. It had got through the "impregnable" net. The destroyer dropped a depth charge and blew the submarine high out of the water. It reminded Bob of the jack rabbits' death throes back in the state of Washington.

Within days, Bob was recalled into the Army, and again given an honorable discharge for having a dependent mother. This time he went to work for a private shipyard at Pier 2 in Honolulu. There was a groundswell of antagonism toward Japanese-Americans as a result of the Pearl Harbor attack. However, there was a great shortage of skilled defense workers and most of them in Hawaii at the time were Japanese-Americans. So they were feared, suspected, resented, disliked, even hated—but in great demand.

Though he was a skilled welder by now, and a key man, Bob had to wear a black badge like the other Japanese-Americans. An armed Coast Guardsman stood over them as they worked, to prevent sabotage. They were given the hardest, dirtiest jobs; Bob often worked in the bilges. But there was no talk of sending him off to a relocation camp on the Mainland as was done to other innocent, patriotic Japanese-Americans.

CHAPTER 6

SETTLING DOWN

After the Pearl Harbor attack, people in Hawaii feared the Japanese were coming back to bomb them again at any moment. There were several false alarms. Rumors abounded. The Islands were under strict military rule with curfews and blackouts. Poor Yoshi, who had come over to Oahu to visit her daughter, just before the attack, got stranded for the duration. She was still technically an alien even after all those years on Kauai, and the authorities would not allow aliens to travel, period.

Bob was working as a welder, and starting to earn good money. There was plenty of overtime. He too was living with his sister. He and a friend bought a house in the Kaimuki section of Honolulu for $5,000, and his mother came to live with him. Bob was putting down roots.

Friends introduced him to Shizuko Uchima, a beautiful girl who was working at a large government office in Honolulu. Sparks flew between them even before he discovered she was also from Kauai, from an Okinawan-

Japanese family. He courted her in earnest and within a few months they were married at the Church of the Crossroads on University Avenue where she sang in the choir. Bob had been raised as a Buddhist but didn't mind converting to Christianity because Buddhists love everyone and are friendly toward other religions. At least in Hawaii. And he was far from devout.

Bob then had both wife and mother in the same house which sometimes put him in a quandary. He loved them both and couldn't favor one over the other.

A happy event was the birth of his one and only child, a daughter named Martha-Ann. She was the apple of his eye and he loved being a father. A sad event was when Yoshi died, and was buried in the Japanese cemetery on Nuuanu Avenue in Honolulu. Bob's brother later had their father, who was buried on Kauai, exhumed, cremated and brought to Oahu, where his ashes were placed alongside Yoshi's.

One of Bob's passions was attending the weekly boxing matches promoted by "Sad Sam" Ichinose who became known in major gyms throughout the world. For more than 50 years, nearly every boxing champion Hawaii produced was trained, managed or promoted by Ichinose. He was posthumously inducted into the International Boxing Hall of Fame and Museum in June, 2000, which pleased Bob no end.

Plenty of work, decent pay, a nice home and family—was Bob happy and satisfied? Not with his unpredictable nature. He was repairing the rusty hull of a container ship at a Honolulu Harbor shipyard when he had a fight with his boss and quit, just like that. He must have been

Friends introduced Bob to Shizuko Uchima. She was also from Kauai, but working in Honolulu. Sparks flew between them.

Bob and Shizuko were married at the Church of the Crossroads.

in a cranky mood because he went home and had a fight with Shizuko, too, while he was at it.

He still had his AB card, so he went to the union hall and passed a test though he had been away from the sea for some time. He immediately signed on with a Merchant Marine ship headed to Baltimore through the Panama Canal, a 45-day trip. He was gone the very next day.

When departing Honolulu Harbor, his ship glided by the shipyard where his friends were hard at work. They were dumfounded to see him waving from the deck the day after he had quit, on his way to distant shores.

His spirits lifted once he was out to sea. As for his wife, well, she probably needed a rest from her temperamental husband.

The crew played poker day and night to while away the time. It was "Deal 'em out!" through the Panama Canal, lock by lock; "Shuffle 'em good!" when they emerged into the Caribbean; "Are you in or out?" as they passed the Florida Keys; and "Who's hiding all the money?" when they reached Cape Hatteras. Cash was getting scarce by then. One reason was that Bob was stashing away his winnings in his locker, not telling anyone. By the time the ship reached Baltimore, he had saved nearly $400.

Here he was, on the East Coast at last. Where to go first? To the legendary Big Apple, of course. He and a bosun's mate he thought was his friend took a train to New York City. Bob had to hide because the bosun got drunk and turned mean. He tried to throw Bob off the train!

Bob stored his belongings in a locker at Grand Central Station, hung onto his poker money, and took the subway to Chinatown; he longed for a good bowl of rice. Then he headed for Harlem, and Sugar Ray Robinson's bar. There had been a lot of publicity about the famous prize fighter's place and it lived up to its reputation.

A friendly black chap helped him find a room and stole the money in his wallet while he slept, carefully leaving the change. Bob thought he was a courteous thief. He kept most of his money right on his person so he could afford to be nonchalant.

He spent four happy days in the city, taking excursion buses to see the sights. Then he went to the union hall to line up another Merchant Marine job. There he met an old buddy from his CCC days on Kauai who knew of an opening for a steward on the *Queen Mary*. Not Bob's cup of tea.

He hopped a bus to Los Angeles and hung out in Little Tokyo for a while. The rice was great. Next he went down to San Pedro and signed on with the S.S. *Sappa-Creek*, a huge oil tanker headed for Saudi Arabia.

The ship stopped at Pearl Harbor and Bob couldn't resist calling Shizuko. She was so happy to hear from him, he went to see her. One thing led to another. She convinced him to stay home.

The ship sailed off to Saudi Arabia without him.

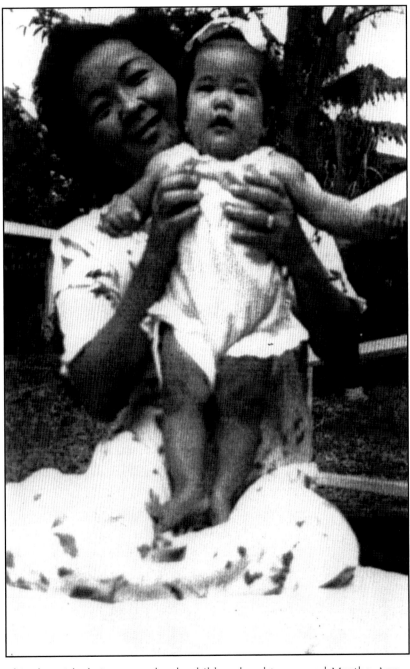

Shizuko with their one and only child, a daughter named Martha-Ann, or "Marti."

CHAPTER 7

THAT OLD FEELING

Bob had bought out his friend, the co-owner of his house, and was on his way to becoming what Yoshi had always wanted him to be, a solid citizen. But by 1955, at age 45, he was getting restless. He longed for variety and wide open spaces. Hawaii was too remote and small.

He also wanted to improve his speech. He had grown up speaking Hawaiian Pidgin, a simplified mixture of English, Chinese, Japanese and Hawaiian, with a little Portuguese and Filipino thrown in. It was wonderfully vivid and expressive, but only a local dialect. Pidgin English might as well as have been Greek outside of Hawaii where nobody understood it. His wife and daughter spoke better English than he did.

He persuaded Shizuko to move to the Mainland where there was more of everything. He went ahead, to scout locations, while she stayed home with their little girl. Later, they joined him. Their Mainland phase lasted 17 years.

First Bob tried Chicago, where he found a job in a

factory, welding air conditioning cabinets, day after day. Not the type of heavy-duty pipe welding he was so good at. Picky stuff. Boring, in fact. He didn't like the city itself, either. Couldn't see bringing his family there.

He lived in a Polish neighborhood near Pulaski Street, named after the Polish count and patriot who was a general in the American Revolutionary War. The neighborhood's only other claim to fame was that it was near the theater where John Dillinger, Public Enemy Number One, was ambushed and shot dead by G-Men (federal agents) in 1934. He was betrayed by the infamous "Woman in Red." People were still talking about it over 20 years later.

So Bob quit Chicago after three months and headed for Seattle, a city he knew pretty well from his days in the Merchant Marine, and felt more optimistic about. The union took him in and he stayed in a housekeeping room. Then he set about working very hard, expanding his welding skills and making some serious money.

Prior to World War II, Japanese-Americans owned and operated most of the housekeeping hotels, as they were called. Many were sent to relocation camps during the war, and other managers operated the hotels for them while they were gone. When the rightful owners returned, they found no maintenance had been performed and the properties badly needed renovation.

It was an intense period in Bob's life. Welders had to be versatile, ready to work at different locations. They were held to strict standards by the contractors, and tested for every job, some of which lasted for months. Bob did pipe welding, primarily, for widely-varying

In 1955, the Okazaki family moved to Seattle, where there was more work. His fellow welders started calling him "Hawaii Kai" for his speed, after Henry Kaiser's hydroplane, then one of the fastest boats in the world.

industrial jobs such as at a paper mill, factory sites, refineries, a huge gas pipeline, on several big new planes for Boeing, and even a sawmill in the southwest.

Bob rubbed elbows with history when he worked in Kelso, Washington, and Longview, Oregon, along the majestic Columbia River. The work involved small pipelines distributing gas to homes. He was close to the famed Oregon Trail where pioneers had endured incredible hardships as they traveled west. He was also near Mount St. Helens, the volcano which later blew its top and sides so cataclysmically, day was like night in downtown Portland.

Bob and a supervisor were once sent to New Mexico, to renovate a sawmill on a Navajo reservation at Shiprock. They experienced radical extremes in weather on the way, going from snow in the mountains to the desert heat. He lived in a trailer provided by the company.

On weekends, he and a friend drove into Gallup to buy beer. It was illegal to sell alcoholic beverages on the reservation, and they wouldn't serve Indians at bars in town, either. But despite the restrictions, alcoholism was a serious problem with the Indians.

It was a problem for Bob, too, a different kind of problem, because the bartenders thought he was a Native American, and didn't want to serve him, either. They had never seen a Japanese-American from Hawaii before.

On the reservation, the Navajos kept sheep which they moved from time to time, rotating pastures. There were no proper gates; they would simply take down a length of wire fencing to let the animals through and put it back up again. The network of roads ran all through the pastures.

Bob was returning from a beer run in Gallup with his pal at the wheel, both somewhat drunk, when the car suddenly came upon a flock of sheep just over a hill, and plowed into the poor creatures, killing around a dozen. It shocked the men sober fast. Bob felt horrible to see the bloody mess.

The outraged Navajo shepherd yelled at him, "How could you do this to *your own people?*," mistaking him for another Navajo. Bob and the driver made amends as best they could.

Later on, when the Navajos got to know him better, they came to him with a suggestion: "Why don't you marry a nice Navajo girl, and have your own homestead here in the desert with us?"

He was flattered, but, thinking of Shizuko and little Martha-Ann, or "Marti," politely refused. Besides, he wasn't that fond of sheep.

Bob was a qualified journeyman, certified for electric and gas welding. He was also very fast. His fellow welders started calling him "Hawaii Kai" for his speed, after industrialist Henry Kaiser's hydroplane, then making news as one of the fastest boats in the world. The nickname stuck.

Contractors would request "Hawaii Kai." For years, mail addressed to "Hawaii Kai" would get to him wherever he happened to be, even in Alaska. He stood out anyway because he was usually the only Japanese-American on the job, as well as one of the fastest welders.

At last he sent for Shizuko and Marti. They rented out the Honolulu house, put their household goods in storage, and moved into a building with housekeeping rooms where Shizuko could manage the property. It was winter and they saw their first snow.

Bob became ambitious, now that he was earning substantially more. He bought a car. He mortgaged the Honolulu house and looked around for a home in Seattle. Once again, he encountered a certain amount of racial prejudice. It was subtle in the state of Washington, but it was still there, an aftermath of World War II. It meant they wouldn't be accepted in certain areas. An open-minded real estate agent found them a suitable duplex residence in the Ballard district, at Crown Hill, which they bought. Ballard had been settled by Norwegians originally, who kept their fishing boats there. Bob and Shizuko got their things out of storage, moved in, and found most of their neighbors friendly and agreeable. The duplex proved a good investment, earning them rental income which helped pay the mortgage.

Marti was the only Japanese-American in the schools she attended for several years. Since she was an only child, she was accustomed to being unique.

The most frightening thing during those years happened at the piano teacher's when Marti was taking a lesson. She backed up to a portable heater and her clothing caught fire. Another piano student, a quick-thinking girl, somehow rushed her into a bathtub and ran water on her, putting out the flames and saving her life. Her back was badly burned, from shoulder to buttocks, and her suffering tore at her parents' hearts.

Tender, loving care and youthful vitality healed her damaged skin eventually, and Marti became her healthy, active self once more.

Bob and Shizuko enjoyed a second honeymoon when they joined a group from Seattle taking a three-week European tour. It appealed to his love of geography. They started in London and hit all the high spots from Amsterdam to Berlin to Rome to Paris, and in-between, traveling around on comfortable buses. Everything was pre-arranged for them, and capable guides traveled with them. Not to worry if they couldn't speak French, German or Italian. The guides could.

At last he saw Switzerland and the Alps. Checked out awesome cathedrals and museums everywhere. Experienced dreamy gondola rides in Venice. Cruised the legendary Rhine on a riverboat. Craned his neck at the Michelangelo dome in St. Peter's Basilica. Visited the impressive Vatican, the Sistine Chapel, the dark, dank catacombs, the Colosseum ruins. Glimpsed Mt. Vesuvius from Naples. Took in the elegant casino at Monte Carlo. (Looked, but didn't gamble.) Ended up in Paris for four days. Admired the Eiffel Tower and the Arc de Triomphe. Pretty heady stuff for a kid from Kauai.

They had been invited to stay in Germany with an Army pal from Hawaii and his wife. By then they had made such good friends with so many members of the group, it was hard to leave the tour. But it was an opportunity not to be missed. They took a train from Paris to Germany, were met by their Hawaiian friends, and treated to several days of private sightseeing and hospitality.

Bob and Shizuko brought home presents, souvenirs, photos and travel adventure tales galore to Seattle and Marti. They had fun keeping in touch with their tour group buddies for many years afterwards, reliving their once-in-a-lifetime European vacation.

A Coast Guardsman neighbor devised an unusual oceanography project for Marti and her school chums. He gave them each an empty bottle with a cork. The youngsters wrote notes, including their names and addresses, and placed them in the bottles. They had fun, pretending to be shipwrecked on a deserted island like Robinson Crusoe.

The Coast Guardsman planned to drop the bottles overboard, one by one, on his ship's next patrol from Seattle to Alaska. Where and when the floating bottles would reach land was anybody's guess. It made the youngsters more aware of the interaction of ocean currents, winds, tides, waves, storms, and just plain luck. They wondered where their bottles were for months afterwards.

Nearly 10 years later, long after Marti had forgotten about hers, she received a letter from a girl on Kauai saying she had found Marti's note in the bottle! It had floated thousands of miles to Hanamaulu Beach where Bob had hung out and fished so often in his Huckleberry Finn days.

CHAPTER 8

ALASKAN ADVENTURES

While it's true Bob was based in the Seattle area for 17 years, he worked in Alaska about 10 different times during that period, at different locations and projects. And he never did set eyes on a bear!

Welders were the stars of all the skilled workers, there was such a shortage of them in Alaska. They wouldn't even accept a job through the union hall back in Seattle unless they were offered "five 10s," "six 10s," "six 12s" or "seven 12s." This referred to the number of days in a week and hours per day. They insisted on a great deal of overtime before leaving home and traveling so far.

A man could earn $2,000 a week plus housing and meals under these terms. The pay scale was at least 40 percent higher than in Seattle. But you could get burnout if you weren't careful. Bob sent most of his pay back home to Shizuko who, like many Japanese-American wives, was the family financial manager. She refused to move to Alaska, so he went back and forth.

By the time he headed north, as a skilled journeyman

welder, Bob knew just about everything concerning
pipeline welding: fabrication, cutting, fitting, and especially angles. Competing with men from the oil fields in
Texas and Oklahoma, who had become skilled welders
while still in their teens, kept him on his toes. He
worked from one end of the state to another, always
with his own helper.

Working conditions were very different from those in
Seattle. Way out at the end of the Aleutian Islands
chain, where he worked several times, there were no
civilian residents, only military people at an air base,
and plenty of foxes. The weather was so severe, the rain
and snow blew *horizontally*.

Planes from the Orient would stop there first to
refuel before flying on to Anchorage. Bob was permit-
ted to go onboard one plane he never forgot. A dedicated benefactor from Portland had made it his per-
sonal mission to round up needy orphans in Asia and
bring them to America for adoption. They included
toddlers and babies. His daughters helped him care for
the children on the long flights. Bob boarded the plane
while it rested on the airstrip, and the sight of dozens
of little ones, hopefully embarking on a better life,
moved him deeply.

On big jobs, he lived in trailer-type houses and ate
free meals in a central kitchen. The food had to be first
class or the union workers would strike. They had
baked ham every Thursday on one job, he fondly
recalled.

His jobs in Alaska included pipeline welding for the
Valdez tank farm. Valdez is a name that lives in infamy

Bob worked in Alaska around 10 different times while based in Seattle.

because of a massive oil spill after Bob worked there that seriously contaminated the pristine harbor, its shoreline and its wildlife. The clean up continued for years.

Bob acquired strange tidbits of information when he worked on Kodiak Island for a new cannery specializing in king crab. King crabs cannot walk on shore; they're too heavy. And someone named Wakefield was first to find out they were good to eat, which led to a whole new industry.

It was a big renovation project involving an existing area built on the piers. Bob and his helper led a team of four installing all the piping for the refrigeration area. In those days, ammonia was the only refrigerant.

There was a lot of male bonding and camaraderie among the workers in Alaska. Bob made one of his best friends ever during this time. The men worked hard and drank hard; there wasn't much else to do.

Bob did go clamming at a nearby island with an electrician buddy. They roasted panfuls of clams in an old wood-burning stove's oven; when the shells popped open, they feasted.

Once in a while his superintendent took him for a ride to a canyon that reminded him of Waimea Canyon on Kauai, except that it was full of evergreens unlike trees in Hawaii. Being more of a lover than a shooter, Bob didn't join his boss in target practice with a pistol, the real object of the trip.

Bob was the only Japanese-American in Kodiak and everyone thought he was an Eskimo, even the Eskimos. When he worked around Indians, they too thought he was one of them and made him welcome. He fit in wherever he went, one way or another.

At Pelican, his helper was an Indian, and Bob got to know the local Tlingits well enough to go fishing and drinking with them. They showed him how to make an unusual kind of pupu. During herring spawning season, the Indians cut branches from the forest, and placed them amid the kelp in the harbor water for a couple of days. The schools of herring literally covered the submerged branches with eggs, as they did the kelp. (The fish didn't know the difference.) Thousands, maybe millions of tiny whitish eggs.

Next, his Indian pals built a fire, heated water in a clean kerosene can, and topped it off with a layer of seal oil, their favorite sauce. They fished a branch from the harbor, broke off smaller sections, dunked them quickly in and out of the hot water to cook the eggs, and added the final touch—the seal oil—on the way out. Bob learned to pull the egg-laden stick through his teeth to remove the eggs and oil, and swallow the tasty concoction while having a beer.

A big job on the Kenai Peninsula saw Bob connecting 20-inch steel pipes from oil-drilling platforms way out in the ocean to a new tank farm that was being built. The pipeline ran underwater and surfaced on shore. That's where the fun began for Bob and dozens of other workers.

A ditch had been dug to receive the pipeline once it had been welded, X-rayed, rustproofed with resin or tar, wrapped, and lowered by boom into the ditch. Bob and his helper worked on 10-20 foot lengths held in

In Shemya, at the far end of the Aleutian Islands, the weather was so severe, the rain and snow blew *horizontally*. Bob, left, with inspector.

wooden cradles alongside the ditch. You had to be extremely careful; deadly accidents on similar jobs had occurred in California and Washington.

Once the pipeline was lowered, it was covered with soil. The job lasted around three hectic months.

Being a perfectionist, as well as speedy, Bob would concentrate intently on each weld, trying to make it better than the last. He was always well aware that it had to pass an X-ray, but he was really competing with himself. He could weld in six minutes what would take another skilled man at least twice as long. Word of his dexterity got around, and the superintendent of the entire job came by to observe him in action.

When a tidal wave hit the coast, caused by a serious earthquake at Anchorage, Bob was working on another refrigeration job for a cannery in Pelican, near Juneau. He had arrived on a small seaplane which skimmed the harbor water in a thick fog, alarming him considerably. What if it crashed headfirst into an oncoming fishing boat? The bush pilots were daredevils compared to commercial airline pilots.

Pelican was located in a fjord, and all the buildings were on piles, 30 feet out from the steep cliffs. Even the cannery was on pilings. The people there knew nothing of the earthquake and ensuing tidal wave until the water in the fjord suddenly emptied out completely, all the way down to the bottom. Astonished otters were scrambling around in the bare mud. It was a sight to see!

People finally realized there had been a big earthquake somewhere fairly close by. Because of the fjord-like formation, the tidal wave itself had not come roaring into Pelican, but had sucked the water out of the harbor, instead, when it receded, as tidal waves do. The water finally returned slowly, and people learned via radio that Anchorage had been devastated.

Bob was employed at the time by a Seattle refrigeration company which sent him to the jobs in Alaska. They told him not to come home when they got news of the earthquake, knowing he would be needed there, but he came anyway because he missed his family. He had barely been home a day when he was sent back to Kodiak, via Anchorage. So he got a first-hand view of the frightful damage at the epicenter itself.

He saw a huge crevasse which divided buildings on a main downtown street dramatically; those on one side had sunk to roof level as the earth under them had cracked open and dropped.

Kodiak was also badly hit. Bob observed big boats cast like toys way up on land, so far from the water they had to dig canals to float them back where they belonged. He found enormous steel bolts, which connected piping to heavy tanks in the cannery receiving room, had actually *stretched* from the force of the tidal wave. Stretched, but not broken.

Ammonia gas had leaked into the holding room where valuable boxes of frozen solid king crab meat were stored. They had been condemned by the Board of Health, and couldn't be sold, even though only those nearest the leak might have been contaminated by the ammonia. The boss told the employees to help themselves to the good boxes. Bob shipped so much frozen crab meat home to Shizuko, she had to have a butcher

Everyone thought Bob, center, was an Eskimo, even the Eskimos!

A truck with welding equipment preceded the welders. Every single weld had to be X-rayed to make sure it was flawless.

A deep trench was dug to receive the pipeline once it had been welded, x-rayed, rustproofed with resin or tar, and wrapped. Then it was lowered by boom into the trench.

with a saw divide the large icy blocks, so she could share them with their neighbors.

Construction workers in Alaska risked life and limb every day, and Bob was no exception. His luck ran out when he broke his back in Kodiak. This was on a different job for the king crab company, building an elevator shaft embedded into the ocean floor.

He was bracing angle irons when improperly fastened bolts gave way and he fell into the shaft, fracturing several vertebrae. The pain was excruciating. He couldn't move. An ambulance arrived quickly and the medics skillfully extricated him. He spent three weeks in a body cast at Kodiak Hospital before he could be flown home to Seattle. When his back healed enough, he graduated to a brace. He had to take six months off, but the company faithfully sent him his weekly pay.

Before he went back to work, he and his family took a long motor trip across the country to Kansas to visit Shizuko's brother. Bob was looking for cowboy territory on the way. A high point of the journey was visiting Mesa Verde National Park in southwest Colorado. Instead of frontier towns, they found sheer cliffs, a trail leading to a high plateau, and prehistoric ruins left by ancient cliff dwellers. It was a memorable interlude of togetherness for the little family.

Bob had more bad luck in remote Shemya, far out at the end of the Aleutians. As he was working with a boom operator, guiding airborne pipe into a ditch, the boom's brakes suddenly slipped and the heavy pipe fell on his leg, breaking it in seven places. It was splinted at the job site and he was given pain killers, but he had to wait *two days* for a plane to Seattle where he was met by an ambulance.

The worried doctor said he might have to amputate. Bob begged him to try and save the leg, and the doctor did. Bob then had to take a year off to recover, and the company paid him his regular wages every week. His bones knit so well he didn't even limp.

But it was the hard way to get all that time off with pay.

They had to be extremely careful; deadly accidents had occurred on similar jobs.

Bob was especially proud of his "offsets," 90 degree elbows.

CHAPTER 9

BACK TO THE FUTURE

A lot happened during those 17 years the Okazakis lived in the Seattle area. Bob came and went. Shizuko made new friends, became part of the community, ran the household, and raised their daughter. Marti grew up, graduated from high school and college, and became a teacher in California. Then, as Fate would have it, they all ended up back in Hawaii.

In 1971, Bob was working for Massart, a major contractor in the Pacific Northwest and Alaska, who wanted to expand to Hawaii. He was offered a good deal to return to Oahu and do gas pipeline work for a new North Shore resort, Del Webb's Kuilima. It was built with the hope it would become Hawaii's first gambling casino.

Work went so well, Massart asked him to run more Hawaii jobs. Out to Hawaii Kai he went, to put in gas lines at the new Koko Marina Shopping Center. After that, it was replacing rusted and corroded pipes along the Waialae Country Club in Kahala, home of the famous annual Hawaiian Open. Hawaii was enjoying a building boom in the seventies, and there was plenty of work for Bob.

He liked being back so much, he sent for Shizuko to pack up and return. He admitted he wasn't much help to her, he was so busy working. Massart paid all moving expenses. They still owned their Kaimuki house, and didn't have to go house hunting. Out went the tenants and in they moved.

When Massart sent Bob to Kalaheo, Kauai, to work on a 50-unit housing development, he drove the company truck around to all the old familiar places. The blacksmith shop where he had worked as a boy was still operating; a welding shop was there, too. He still knew many of the men, who were happy to "talk story" with him, and a little impressed to think he had been sent to Kauai by a mainland company.

Massart tried very hard to get established in Hawaii, but the union was against them. They got fed up and moved the Hawaii office to Guam. Bob had no interest in moving to hot, humid Guam, so he said aloha to Massart and had no trouble finding another job.

His next project was a challenge worthy of a man at the top of his game. With a foreman and a helper, Bob took on what they called the stadium pipeline job, although it had nothing to do with the stadium. They were installing an oil pipeline from Red Hill to Pearl Harbor that ran along the stadium's perimeter.

Bob welded big 16-inch pipes and was especially proud of his "offsets," 90 degree elbows. As usual, every weld was X-rayed. Even a pinpoint defect could be spotted. It was flattering that those in charge expected him to handle the most complicated segments. The company had sought him out, waited for him to become available, and were paying him a dollar an hour over scale to show their appreciation.

He was a trim, fit 62 years of age, working at a tank farm near Sand Island Bridge, when he decided to quit while he was ahead. He announced that he was retiring, and retire he did.

It was time to smell the flowers and ponder the future.

CHAPTER 10

MORE LIVES THAN A CAT

Ever resourceful, Bob changed direction drastically and took up oil painting. He attended an art class and produced a series of landscapes, often depicting the beaches and ocean in Hawaii. Shizuko also studied art. Her taste ran to more formal, oriental-style paintings of flowers. She got the urge to travel more, now that she had some free time, and joined tours to Australia, New Zealand, Hong Kong and Japan while Bob was doing his thing in Hawaii.

Marti expressed her creativity by getting married and having four children: Rhonda, David, Corey and Jason. Bob and Shizuko loved being grandparents and were very close to the children. They often took them to and from school. Fed them, played with them, kept them overnight and longer. Bob's fondest memories were of taking them to the beach every chance he got when they were young.

When Rhonda was a child, she belonged to a hula halau (school of dance) that was invited to perform in Japan. They were accompanied by Hawaiian singers and musicians. Bob went along to help chaperone his

little granddaughter, of whom he was very proud, and
see his parents' homeland. He still spoke the language
but found his accent puzzled and amused the native
Japanese.

Little Rhonda was chosen to announce the perform-
ances and memorized a proper speech in Japanese.
They performed in Osaka and Disneyland, which was
just like the one in California except for the food. They
visited shrines, a big castle with a moat, and an apple
orchard which reminded Bob of his apple-picking days
in Washington.

Bob discovered he felt no more genetic or psychic con-
nection to Japan and its people than he had experienced
in Europe. He figured it was from being brought up in eth-
nically diversified Hawaii where they called the racial mix-
tures from so many intermarriages "chop suey." He realized he was American through and through.

On the side, Bob air-brushed designs on cars for
friends, did body and fender work in his garage for
other friends, and planted dieffenbachias by the dozen
in his backyard in Kaimuki. He didn't worry about
where all this might lead to, but lived for the moment
and took every day as it came.

When a pal leased five acres to start a nursery in
Waimanalo, a rural area on Oahu, Bob's welding skills
were needed once more. Pipes were delivered from Texas
to use for strong posts. Not for fencing, but for cables to
hold up heavy plastic shade cloth, which came in 20-foot
squares. It filtered the brilliant Hawaiian sunshine and
protected the plants from sunburn. Bob welded cable
holders onto the tops of each post.

Back in Hawaii, after 17 years on the Mainland, Bob retired and took up oil painting. Marti got married and had four children: Rhonda, David, Corey and Jason. Bob and Shizuko loved being grandparents.

Bob began collecting bromeliads and fell extravagantly in love with them. His collection soon outgrew his backyard.

Gradually, he added bromeliads to his backyard plantings at home. People began coming by to see them and talk story about gardening. He often gave away seedlings and, though he hated to part with them, once in a while would sell a larger plant. The small scale hobby grew by word of mouth and evolved into a small business before Bob realized what was happening. He had never even heard of an invoice, and knew nothing of business procedures, sales or marketing.

Meanwhile, he fell extravagantly in love with bromeliads. He kept on buying and growing more all the time. More Aechmeas, more Cryptanthus, more Tillandsias, and more Neoregelias (his favorites).

He was one of the founders of the Hawaii Bromeliad Society. He produced bromeliad exhibitions for the annual Orchid Show in Blaisdell Center, taking several first prizes. Pretty soon he was showing off his darlings at hotel fashion shows, musical events, charity fundraisers, and craft fairs, too.

He was invited to attend a two-week conference on bromeliads in Australia, at Townsville in Queensland, where he learned a lot about propagation and hybridization, and made many new friends.

In Australia, he stayed with a prominent bromeliad dealer and her family who owned gigantic cattle ranches, complete with cowboys, in several locations. It took two company helicopters to keep in touch with the far-flung operations.

After the conference, his Australian friends flew him to one of their ranches where they all stayed in the big ranch house, and dined together with 12 to 15 at a sitting. He was shown around the spread which had cisterns to catch and hold rain water. He saw where they branded and gelded calves. He was intrigued by the wide expanses of deep grass which was full of invisible kangaroos—invisible until they popped their heads up to take a look around. Flocks of beautiful parrots wheeled through the sky in formation. You could see for miles in every direction.

Bob was a novelty to the cowboys who had never met a Japanese-American. They put him on a horse and wanted him to go with them to round up some cattle. He stayed on the beast only long enough to have his picture taken, then fell off and stayed off. He had often ridden horses back on Kauai as a boy, but it wasn't fun any more.

Before he returned, he bought two irresistible Papillon puppies, toy spaniels with silky coats and large, erect ears held so they resembled the wings of a butterfly. One was black and white; the other brown and white. They had to spend three months in quarantine in Honolulu before he could bring them home because of a strict regulation designed to keep rabies out of the Islands. It bothered Bob more than the dogs, and he visited them every day so they wouldn't forget him.

One conference led to another, as his passion for bromeliads grew. He was the first from Hawaii to make the rounds of these conferences. Off he went to Los Angeles and Houston, and then to New Orleans and Bourbon Street, where he met and partied with some wild and crazy Aussies he had met previously Down

Bob was invited to a bromeliad conference in Australia. Afterwards, he was a guest at a big ranch where the cowboys put him on a horse to go round up cattle. But he fell off, instead, and stayed off.

Bob made the rounds of many other conferences. In Florida, he took a side trip deep into the Everglades jungle. There he spied monkeys gone wild after being imported for the filming of a Tarzan movie.

He could see large, scary alligators only too close on the banks of the small stream.

Under. Vendors from all over began to recognize and greet him.

A major conference in Florida was especially exciting. Bob took a side trip deep into the Everglades jungle, with a diver looking for artifacts from prehistoric times when the ocean covered the entire swamp.

They wended their way up a long narrow stream in a motorboat. Monkeys, who had escaped into the wild and multiplied, chattered and capered in the trees. Bob could see large scary alligators only too close on the banks. The diver was unconcerned. He stopped the boat where the stream was shallow and dove into the clear water, bringing up fossilized treasures such as the giant shark's tooth and the Indian arrowhead Bob brought home to Hawaii.

Bob developed an international network of contacts among bromeliad dealers, including some in Taiwan and Thailand. He got a permit to import plants. Word got around. More bromeliad enthusiasts began coming to him, asking him to order certain plants for them. Some were large, unusual plants called Medallions, worth $500 and more apiece. Some large Imperials were worth as much as $2,000 each!

Other devotees found out about him and came to see him when they were in Hawaii. Visitors came from Europe, Australia and New Zealand, as well as the Mainland.

Since he was bursting out of his backyard, he leased a couple of acres of agricultural land in Kahaluu, and became a prominent bromeliad supplier. Among his customers were the Waikiki Sheraton hotels and the

Hilton Hawaiian Village, largest resort in the Pacific Basin. His customer base kept expanding. And he never spent a cent on advertising.

For Bob, retirement meant he turned into a combination retailer, wholesaler, plant broker and horticulturist. He simply added these new occupations to his previous jobs:

Certified Welder,
Journeyman Pipefitter,
Able-Bodied Seaman,
Sandblaster,
CCC camp cook,
Army cook,
Stone quarry worker,
Breakwater builder,
Tunnel digger,
Apple picker,
Hops plucker,
Blacksmith,
Fisherman,
Grape stomper,
Sugar cane measurer,
Canefield weed chopper.

There were probably some others, here and there, but those were just the ones he remembered.

He was one of the founders of the Hawaii Bromeliad Society, and displayed his treasures at annual garden shows.

Chapter 11

The Cutting Edge

When the Millennium rolled around, Bob found himself on the cutting edge of the fastest-growing segment of the U.S. population. These remarkable Golden Oldies were hardy and tough. They still worked every day. They had the right stuff.

On the other hand, poor Shizuko developed heart trouble and died at the age of 79, leaving Bob torn with sorrow, wishing he had been able to prevent her suffering. He went to her grave almost every day, telling her he would soon be joining her. But he was mistaken.

At 90, he was still running his own house, enjoying his backyard bromeliads, raising a new Papillon puppy in addition to Marti's little white Maltese dog Coco, and greeting visitors who came by to see his private collection, talk story and drink beer.

He loved his daily Korean TV soap operas. He zipped into Zippy's for lunch and gave the waitress friendly pats on the bottom. He kept in touch with his grandchildren and extended family. Kept up on the current news.

Reporters learned of his bromeliad passion, and he

was featured on TV and in the newspaper. Old buddies on Kauai were thrilled to read about him and see his photo. He received dozens of phone calls and visits.

Bob gradually gave up his elaborate exhibitions and the nursery in Kahaluu. He finally stopped going to mainland conferences. He quit driving at age 89 after he totaled his car and walked away without a scratch. He sported a jaunty cast after he broke his wrist taking Coco for a walk at three o'clock in the morning. It healed up quickly.

Bob was often compared to the Energizer Bunny, a pink, drum-beating mechanical toy featured in TV commercials, eternally chugging across the screen, demonstrating the long-lasting power of Energizer batteries.

Shizuko was going to have a long wait before the kid from Kauai joined her.

At 90, Bob was raising Marti's little white Maltese dog, Coco, plus a new Papillon puppy, Myke.

Bob was featured in *The Honolulu Advertiser*, Jan. 5, 2001. "Bromeliad Man" was written by Mike Leidemann. Photo by Eugene Tanner.

CHAPTER 12

FAREWELL TOUR

Epilogue

In February 2001, Bob's daughter, Marti, took him and Dorothy Hazzard to Kauai so he could saturate both women with the ambiance of his boyhood home territory. Also for background to his memoir. At age 90, he often proclaimed during the trip that this was his positively last visit to the island of his birth.

By now, Marti had married Robert Hazzard, and Dorothy was her mother-in-law as well as a writer.

Dorothy and Bob Okazaki didn't know what to call their own relationship, if any, so Bob startled people they met on Kauai by introducing her as his "girlfriend." It caused double takes, uproarious laughter, jokes and comments. People weren't sure he meant it, given his reputation for being a rascal. The domino effect took hold, and some of the men came forth with surprising claims that they, too, had girlfriends.

Bob never hesitated to question or guess at a person's ethnic identity, as is the custom with older folk in Hawaii. Nobody resented it; most of the time he was right. Often he would speak to people in their own language. He seemed to know greetings and other phrases in several.

It was raining when they arrived, but they were too excited to care. Number One target was Hanamaulu Bay, Bob's favorite body of water in the whole world. Down they drove in the rented Buick with Marti at the wheel. Soon they were gazing at the Ahukini Landing where Bob had first signed on with the Merchant Marine. It was also the pier the German ship captain had nearly rammed when the ship was picking up a load of sugar. Nearby was the breakwater he barely missed crashing into with poor Bob quaking at the wheel.

The Ahukini Landing had fallen into disrepair. All its planking was gone and only the supporting pillars were left, still standing in the water. The breakwater looked as good as new.

Bob could see things as they used to be, in his mind's eye, and recalled how, in "small kid time," his father took him fishing from the pier, and picking "pipipi," tiny black mollusks, from the rocks along the shore.

Gone was his old house and the whole plantation camp when they got to Hanamaulu itself. This was expected, as one by one the sugar operations on Kauai and throughout Hawaii had closed.

Bob was soon chatting up the staff of the Hanamaulu Cafe, owned by an old friend named Roy, and later by his son. Next door was a Japanese Teahouse where they decided to dine. He and the young waitress hit it off immediately. She answered his

Marti married Robert Hazzard in August, 1999. Between them, they had six children, five of which were boys.

questions, warmly smiling, calling him "Papa," and giving him details of local news. Both spoke colorful pidgin.

When they sat down to dine, near a picturesque Japanese garden, Bob sighed, looked around in an ecstatic daze, and said, "Oh, I've come *all happy!*"

After dinner, rain or darkness nothwithstanding, Bob insisted that they drive down a long, winding road to Hanamaulu Beach, his private version of Paradise. There was a charming park there now, with pavilions for picnicking. The shore was lined with ironwood trees. Cliffs on each side extended to the mouth of the Bay. The beach itself was crescent-shaped, with firm sand, and ideal waves rolling in, one after another, so you could tell that the bottom got deeper gradually instead of suddenly dropping off.

"Perfect for children," Bob said.

It was hard to believe the smallish Bay was 30 feet deep farther out and that a big ship could come in to pick up sugar as it had in the old days.

They parked at the edge of the beach and shone the headlights onto the sand and water. Bob couldn't wait to get rid of his slippers, roll up his trousers, and get his feet into that magic water.

Now that they had done first things first, they registered at the Marriott, a luxurious fantasy resort at Nawiliwili, and slept soundly.

Next day, back to Hanamaulu they traveled, to see it in the sunshine and broad daylight. On a steep hillside, they found the cemetery where Bob had feared the obake. Some of the headstones were leaning as though ghosts had pushed them aside to get out and scare people.

On the way down to the beach, they saw lush green-
ery, mango and guava trees, coconut palms, stands of
banana and papaya, and foundations where houses
had once stood.

Bob wanted to stop at a friend's house, and a chap
who was working out back came around to talk story
with them. The man, in his fifties, proved knowledge-
able about the history of the area and was the son or
grandson of someone Bob had known. His name was
Lester and he couldn't have been more gracious.

He and Bob recalled how the different ethnic groups
stuck together in the old plantation camps. The
Japanese were together here, the Filipinos there, the
Portuguese yonder, the Chinese elsewhere—each group
brought its language, food, religion, clothing styles,
customs and gene pool to Hawaii, adding a hybrid vigor
that enhanced successive generations.

The road passed large, flat, open wetlands on each
side of a small river. This was once carpeted with rice
paddies. Chinese farmers leased the land, enclosing
30 x 30 foot plots with narrow dikes to control the flow
of water. They used water buffaloes to plow, and for
other heavy work. Hence the name for "buffalo grass,"
which grew profusely downriver where Bob sometimes
swam as a boy.

He and his pals firmly believed that the Chinese
always walked single file wherever they went, even in
town, a habit they had formed from walking on the narrow dikes.

Kauai has a good many rivers and each river has a
valley. The Chinese leased the valleys. Japanese women

Marti took her father to Kauai for what he considered his farewell tour.
He couldn't wait to dump his slippers, roll up his trousers, and get his
feet into that magic water.

planted the rice by hand. At harvest time, the paddies were drained. The rice was cut, dried and thrashed to separate the kernels from stalks and leaves. It was a labor-intensive process, as was the sugar industry. The Hawaiians couldn't see any sense in working so hard, and the plantation owners had to import foreign labor.

As memories came flooding back, Bob said that, unbeknown to him, his older brother, Yosuke, had canceled his (Bob's) dual citizenship with Japan, making Bob solely an American. Bob didn't learn of it until much later. Yosuke died early, and Bob was never sure why his brother had done it. He must have thought it was for Bob's own good.

Next they stopped at the Lihue Cafe, to be greeted warmly by Harry Miyake, whose son was running the place now. Harry showed them additions and improvements since Bob was last there. Billiards and poker tables, karaoke—the changes were impressive. The name, Lihue Cafe, was an understatement. "Pleasure Palace" was more like it.

They resumed Bob's farewell tour driving along southern Kauai. Through Puhi, side trip to Koloa, on to Lawai, Kalaheo, Eleele, Hanapepe, and Port Allen. At Waimea, Bob visited his white-haired, soft-spoken cousin, Sumi Munechika. They embraced each other tenderly, perhaps for the last time.

Kekaha was the final stop, at Bob's in-laws. They were Marti's Uncle Shigeru and Auntie Kikue Okihara. Kekaha was Shizuko's original hometown and Kikue was her sister. There was much exchanging of family news plus phone calls to other relatives. Cousin Faith joined them for a festive dinner that night.

Bob was totally exhilarated as host, and regaled his Kauai connections with stories and witticisms. They, in turn, told awesome tales of a hurricane that had ripped off their roof, brought ocean waves far onto the land, reaching their house and beyond, and how they had been evacuated, without power or water for days on end.

After reluctant goodbyes, it was back to the hotel, and to Oahu the next day.

On the plane flying back, Bob began changing his tune. Instead of threatening to join Shizuko in heaven at any moment, Marti and Dorothy heard him musing to himself:

"I'm going to make a party. I'll have an imu, we'll get a pig, I'll cook my famous oxtail soup..." Pretty soon he had the whole menu worked out in his head.

It looked like *party planner* was going to be his next occupation.

Father and daughter enjoyed a return to Hanamaulu Bay, his boyhood playground.

Bob pointed out the river and buffalo grass, where he had so often
swum as a boy, on the way to Hanamaulu Bay, his private version
of Paradise.

About the Co-Author

Dorothy Emery Hazzard attended UNH, married, had three children, wrote feature articles for *New Hampshire Profiles*, became a copywriter in Boston ad agencies for 17 years before moving to Honolulu in 1975. After a tour with VISTA, the domestic Peace Corps, she became a consultant in advertising and public relations. Next, she founded a resume and business writing service, which she operated with partners for 18 years.